Verses from Life

Dr. Manjula Rajan

BookLeaf Publishing
India | USA | UK

Presentation by *BookLeaf Publishing*

Web: www.bookleafpub.com

E-mail: info@bookleafpub.com

ISBN: 9789363317796

First edition 2024

This book is dedicated to my dear parents.

It is also an attempt to awaken the long-buried dreams in all of us, especially women, who can pick up their lives at any age and make a name for themselves.

It is a message for everyone out there not to wallow in self-pity but to take charge of their lives and craft a newer and better world for themselves and their families.

Here's hoping that the poems will ignite a new flame in everyone's life, and may the flame burn brighter and stronger and lead towards more fulfilling paths.

ACKNOWLEDGEMENT

Where would I be without my beautiful parents, who nurtured and taught me the values of life? The trust that they had in me goaded me on to pursue my education after a hiatus of 18 years. But for my father, I would not be the happy and successful teacher I am today.

My husband and children have stood by me during the toughest phases, and I feel truly blessed and grateful for having them in my life. Their constant support helped me sail through several rough patches.

My school, my teachers, and my schoolmates need a very special mention. It was the best school in a small town called Calicut, in Kerala, and the confidence that it instilled in me has been my biggest strength.

In the journey of life, we meet several people. Some friends are like luminant stars, and we glow in their light. I am grateful to my colleagues and friends in many ways.

How can I not acknowledge those people who discouraged me and doubted my ability to go back to college with my son? Every taunt propelled me to new heights, and here I am with my first book of poetry!

I hope every reader will understand and relate to the emotions that are brought out in the book. Happy reading!

PREFACE

This collection is an attempt to bring out the complex emotions we all go through in the course of life. Life is an amalgamation of varied experiences, and poetry is the best way to ease one's heart and mirror the countless emotions one goes through in different stages.

I have always been in awe of Emily Dickinson, and her brief yet powerful writing has influenced me deeply. Poetry has, through the ages, been a medium of expression, especially at the most emotionally charged moments. It has helped many to externalize the inner anguish that rages within and threatens to devour their dreams.

The reader can relate with ease to the thoughts that have been shared in this collection. The emotions in the poems are universal, and the juxtaposition of the fleeting moments of joy with the deep depths of despair is a reflection of life. So, here we go!

Letting Go

Pain weighs us down–
The heart is weary,
Thoughts chase memories–
Together, they slide and drain.

The brain shuts down–
Time freezes in its own,
The world seems empty,
No cheer, no words we hear.

Memories flood our hearts–
A glimpse, a hope from the past,
Chars our soul deeper and darker,
As we stay cocooned in our grief.

Then comes a gentle wind–
Whistling in our ears a plea,
Why hold on to that pain,
Let it go, just let it go.

Loved ones flock around–
A kind word, an embrace,
Time ticks and the heart beats,
It's been long, let it go.

There's no pride, nothing to hide–
Close doors, open your hearts,
Usher in a brand new you,
Bring in cheer, let it just go.

Caught in the Crossfire

Sometimes we are at a crossroad,
Most times at the edge of a precipice.
Or hanging on to dear life,
From a precarious, perilous cliff.

Just when we wish we could let go,
A flicker, a ray, a bird song, or a rustle,
Stirs in our hearts a faint glimmer
Of hope, a faint dream, an impossible wish.

Catch your breath, hold your reins–
It's not the end of the road yet.
A mother's love, a loved one's song
A fond smell from childhood rakes up life's
embers.

Shake off that dread, that useless guilt–
Life has been fairly good, despite the jolts.
You are not yours alone; embrace that love
Folks shower on you because you are you.

When caught in the crossfire of life–
Give it a shake and hold your head high.
Life isn't for the feeble-hearted,
Be the brave heart, the inspiration, the epitome
of life.

Stand tall amidst the invisible dreams–
Stop wallowing in the shadow of doubts.
Look within for that undying flame of faith
March towards new goals, renewed hopes!

The Door to Happiness

We reach out, we search
For the mirage of happiness.
The quest is on and goes on.
We look for wealth and some fame–
To define our idea of happiness.

Stop the search, say the pundits
It's not out there or anywhere.
Why not lay your heart bare?
Look within the deep crevices
Of the chapters of your life.

Why do we bend, why do we break?
Why this quest for happiness?
A kind word, a small gesture,
A loving smile, a helping hand
And your heart hums with happiness

Follow your heart

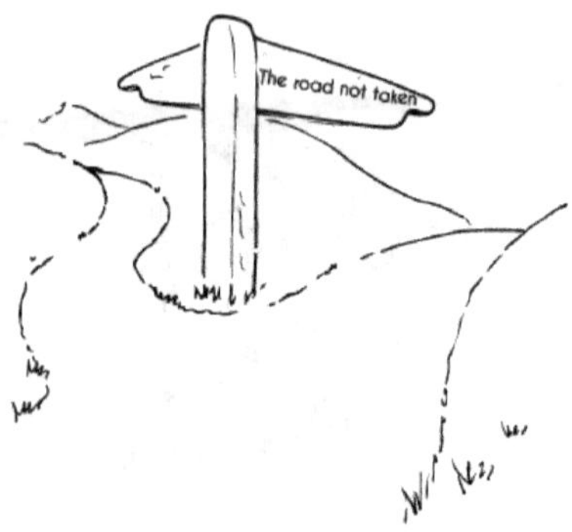

I stood at the crossroads–
Wondering which road to take,
They all looked the same
But had different shores.
I heard a voice say
Just follow your heart.

Then came a passerby–
He said this one is safe.
No troubles, no wars,
It's as calm as the placid seas.
I heard a voice say
Just follow your heart.

I saw a traveler come by–
Down another road.

He said, go up that way,
There's adventure and fun.
I heard a voice say
Just follow your heart.

I strode down the untrodden–
None had passed that way.
I traversed down rocky paths,
And won my dreams down there.
I heard a voice say–
Just follow your heart.

Mother

Her gentle touch, that loving, sometimes stern
look–
Her caring words, the unmeasured love,
She gives it all, unconditional and unending.
Her heart aches when her children defy
Those harsh words she bears with a smile.
No matter what, she stands by our side
Ready to hold, lest we falter and fall.

Her aging shoulder is always on standby–
In case her kids need a wall to lean on.
Prayer after prayer her heart sends,
Seeking peace and good health for them
Who mistake her love for unsolicited concern.
Remember folks, her aging heart
Can not for long play its part.

As long as she is there, we hardly care,
The backlash goes on, as do her unshed tears.
Before long, we miss her kind words, her loving
look–
We wish, oh, how we wish, we had been gentler
With our words and kinder in our deeds.
Pity, it's too late; she is gone, but her voice
lingers–
Her memories haunt, her absence hurts.

We wish we could see her just once–
And seek forgiveness for the seamless hurt,
That drained her heart and parched her life.
We hear afar her gentle voice,
Her footsteps treaded softly.
Come on, folks, let's cherish our dear mothers,
Whose hearts bleed behind those feigned smiles.

Let's give her some love–
As her heart sends out those blessings
That shields us from unforeseen misery.
It's surely not too much to ask–
A little care, a bit of love, a kind word, a gentle
hug
Bring cheer to her weary heart,
And she is the rock, playing her part.
I am sure it's not too much to ask.

A Dream Gone Wrong

We have a deep kindled dream–
However silly it might seem,
It's the beacon of joy and hope,
As we falter, slip, struggle, and grope.

Some say, why have a dream that shatters–
It's your happiness that matters.
Let's be grateful and go with the flow,
Watch out for the blessings that grow.

We strive; we search for that distant dream–
One that lends a purpose and makes us beam.
Oft we reach out for a helping hand,
That navigates us to that dreamland.

When the dream finally fades–
A barrage of emotions mercilessly raids.
Why, oh why have I failed?
Despite the several rough seas sailed.

Some move on, seek a new path–
Many perish in the seething wrath.
And then we hear people kindly say
It's a dream gone wrong; there's another day.

Living on a Bubble

She sails along life's dark, high seas–
Not afraid of the storms.
Wrapped around a shimmering sheath
That shields her from war and words.

She thrives safely within the wrap–
The abuse, the lashes seldom pierce.
It sometimes buoys, sometimes sinks
She lies curled, helpless, yet safe.

None can hear the cries for help–
The bubble seems too vibrant
To appear as a red flag in the voyage of life
She hears the world say, she has it all.

She dare not peer out of the bubble–
As she lies in the depths of life's rubble.
Badly shaken, but not broken–
Wallowing in the depths of her sterile bubble.

Me and Myself

I am no loner,
I love life and banter.
There are folks around–
No, I am in no way bound

There is a tussle in my heart,
As I go around playing my part.
I look around and wonder–
How to sprint across to yonder.

The empty words and hapless lives,
And the placid, painful smiles
The fading façade of happiness,
Reflect life's eerie emptiness.

Amidst the chaos, I stayed afloat
At times I peered within and did gloat
I ticked off my deep and facile flaws
Resolved not to tread the path of pathos

I am me and let me be
A bouquet of imperfections for you to see.
Life is far too gone
Me and myself are not alone.

The Stoked Dreams

The dreams that we see while awake
Need a prod, a good, vigorous shake,
Maybe even a last desperate poke
Like the dying embers that we gently stoke.

Just when we think it's game over,
We tend to hang on for a while longer.
A last plod, a hopeful poke
Before you slump, crumpled and broke

Look for that faint dying strain,
Go for it, despite the piercing pain.
Before long, you see a feeble spark–
When stoked, bursts into flame and leaves its
mark.

Eclipse those moments of disdain,
When you froze and thought it was all in vain.
Cherish that one last desperate tug–
That salvaged you from a perilous choke.

There you are, moving from shadows to light,
You are a winner; you have all the might.
Grateful for that moment, that final stoke
That made you stand out from ordinary folk.

The Mind

The mind is my master,
Day in and day out–
I try to muster,
That inner strength
To dance to its tunes.
Some days are a breeze
On others, I tend to freeze–
I try in vain to keep it at peace.

When the going is good,
My heart goes on a giddy waltz.
Then there are days when a storm rages
That threatened to devour my peace.
My soul shatters, my heart slithers
To a dark corner of hopelessness
My mind, the fighter stands by me
Fights those demons
And places me on a mantle of peace.

It sure is a matter of the mind
That hauls us through the mundane grind.
Let not the demons capture our souls,
Nor make us victims of our own ghouls.
Look within for that treasure trove
Of seamless love, peace and courage–
That always buoys up our undying spirit–
And face the world without a dint.

The lost Time

When I was young,
The days just skipped by–
Weeks turned to months
Months into years
And the years rolled by,
One after one and another one
How I long for the lost time.

And then, as I grew,
Joy and pain joined
The long ride of life.
The happy ones fleeted
The painful ones lingered
Often, joy and sorrow merged
How I long for the lost time.

Now in my twilight,
Memories from the past
Flood my yearning heart.
Sometimes they bring a smile
Sometimes a tear rolls down
Wish I could turn the clock back–
How I long for the lost time.

Stifled Dreams

I was special; I was the firstborn
Showered with love, I was not alone.
Deep in my heart, I too had a dream
Shelved for a new life, as it might seem.

Childhood to motherhood was a leap
A tab over the fleeting years I couldn't keep
Life went on, the commitment grew
My dreams, my passion vanished and flew.

The children grew and so did I–
I waded, I raced, none heard the cry,
Before I perished, I took a perilous turn–
A new start, new candles of hope to burn.

I juggled, I tripped, myself I hauled–
Sometimes I cheered, oft I felt mauled.
A wife, a mother, and many other
None, not one, could guide or gather,

My dreams still lay deeply buried–
As my aimless life raced and hurried
I did what I could to play my part
Aches and dead dreams festered in my heart.

Looking back, I often wonder–
At my foibles, small wins I ponder.
I see a trail of abandoned dreams,
I am too old to pick up, it seems.

None cared to steer or cheer when young–
Now I am told I am old, my dreams too far
flung,
Act your age and carry on your part–
Why do you even want a new start?

Oh my Pot!

It's been a long day, a tiring one too–
I tried to rest, but my mind was in charge,
It refused to shut down or take a nap,
I did what I loved to do most

I walked into that heavenly space–
That part of my home I love most,
And there they were, all lined up
My pots-sparkling and beckoning.

I felt my spirits soar, my fatigue lift
My heart did a waltz to the rhythm of my pots.
My soul joined the dance of joy–
What would I do without you; Oh, my Pots!

The Theorem of Life

Life is a rider–
Has no rule or formula.
It's oft a jagged journey–
With unexpected ups and listless lows.

How we wish we had a handbook of life–
To go to when we are in two minds.
Sometimes we go with the flow,
Other times, we are beaten and just so low.

Google never shows life's path–
Family and friends seldom lead.
Everyone is mired in the aftermath
Listen to your heart, reason with your mind.

Learn to swim against the tide
The mirage of a haven beckons.
Life is a cocktail of hope and despair,
Live in the now; we know not what awaits.

It's not always moonbeams and rainbows–
Dark clouds drift; there sure is a shift.
And then you hear the drum roll,
Voila! You are ready to rock and roll!

You are the captain; you are the anchor–
Hold your head above the stormy waters.
Dare to dream, and pause to cherish–
Life is a rider, has no formula or theorem.

Why am I this way?

The sunshine didn't soothe–
The moonlight didn't ease,
The world just passed by,
No warmth, no smiles–
Cocooned in my thoughts,
The pain in my heart lurks
I heard a cry from within–
Oh why, oh why am I this way?

Friends met and chattered,
None heard the cry within.
The days tunneled past,
The months rolled by–

No kind shoulder to cry,
No hands to lift me up.
I heard a cry from within
Oh why, oh why am I this way?

And then I peered within–
Met my simple soul,
Poured my heart out,
You are your best mate–
Believe in you more and more,
Heard my soul kindly say.
I heard a voice from within–
Yeah, oh yeah, I am happy this way.

Halfway along the Highway

I sped past people, young and old–
Family, friends, and well-wishers, I am told.
We zipped past the known, unknown, and
others–
No time to cheer; none really bothered.

There were roadblocks, sometimes tackled–
Fraught with fear, we oft buckled.
That didn't really put on the brakes
I was ready to give it all that it takes.

Passing by, we seldom stopped–
Quite often, we skipped and hopped,
The young, the old, and the upcoming,
All sped with aimless goals in the coming.

And then came a sudden, unscheduled halt.
Out of nowhere came that bottomless fault.
This too will pass, preached everyone,

Who had passed that way and made the run.

Why not pause and take time to reflect–
Life is short and far from perfect.
Let's care and life's moments share,
Time for our joys and sorrows to be laid bare.

As we race along life's highway,
Look for some sunshine not so far away.
Shed those mighty, glorified dreams–
Come on! Life is not as hard as it seems.

Living a Lie

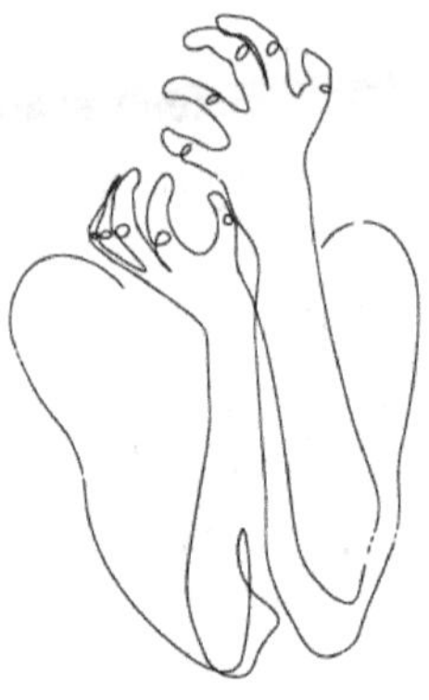

We cheer, we smile, we glow–
A veneer for that piercing pain.
That searing blow that derails life again,
As we pretend to go with the flow.

And then one day, the barrage breaks–
We wish we had somewhere to hide.
We muster courage and the toll it takes,
To break the fall from a deeper slide.

We oft ask ourselves, are we living a lie?
As days fleet, our hearts some solace seek.
Nothing stops; weeks, months, and years fly,
Hoping for the day when resilience peaks.

What then is life if not peril and strife–
Will the façade banish our blues?
We strive to make the best of this life,
Hoping for happier and brighter cues.

Time to Change

Remember those barren days–
When we stagger and laze,
Feeling stagnated, stuck, and rooted–
No pace, no life, badly booted.

We hear a cry, a menacing moan–
None hear the agonizing abysmal groan.
It's time to turn and stir the pot
Never hang on and set the rot.

Shuffle your cards, change your mind–
Shake off the barren, boring grind.
Go for it – that extra meaningful mile,
There you go, with a glow and smile.

Be the pathbreaker, the brave heart–
Feel the stirred dreams, play your part.
Cherish the unfelt, elusive whirlwind wins,
Wear that smile, a new journey begins.

The Pair

They stood side by side–
Made a handsome pair,
Each exudes a charm
What would one be without the other?

Who goes first?
It really doesn't matter.
They are a winning team
And so sought after.

A touch of salt, a dash of pepper–
Make your soups and salads,
The curries, the pastas
Taste so much better.

In the line-up on my kitchen shelf–
They stand supreme and royal
The chili, the mustard
And all the rest are loyal adherents.

They vie with each other
Neither wins hands down.
They complement each other–
They are the royal pair!

The Façade

Imagine a wild world
Without a façade,
A world that knows
The dark, deep secrets–
That lie cuffed and curled up
In a corner of your heart.

We smile, we chat, we share–
None knows the troubled wars
That rage within with no respite.
Some ace the game, some crumble
Most just burst; let the world know
The turbid emotions deep within.

Lucky are those with flawless facades–
Nothing can rake or break the fake,
No wars to fight after the wake,

It could be a loss, an unsolicited love–
Or a daring desire, a nagging failure
The wild pipe dreams buried within.

Why the façade, some ask–
Speak out, come out, open up,
Imagine the anguish of the aftermath,
The murky, turbid waters after the wade.
Rise high, frame that fierce façade,
Hold your secrets, keep that smile.

Gratitude

The small joys of the summer rays–
The aroma of mother's coffee,
The warmth of our homes, our loved ones–
The cozy beds and the loving meals.
Day in and day out, we take for granted,
The love, the care, the comfort, the blessings.

We look around and see the neglect–
The hunger, the thirst, the want,
A sudden guilt assaults our souls,
How blessed are we on the other side.
A glimmer of guilt, a slice of gratitude,
Touches our hearts and makes us humane.

We reach out, we serve, we share,
A sense of brotherhood binds us.

Let nothing be taken for granted–
For destiny might derail our comforts,
While the going is good, let's send out a prayer,
For the love and life we have with us.

A Journey

The prelude to a journey is so much fun–
The boxes, the bags are packed and done.
The gifts, the sweets, the family's participation,
The thrill, the excitement augur anticipation.

A train's window seat brings in more cheer–
We get to see the outside bustle far and near.
A game of cards, mother's delicious packed
meals,
Your favorite book – I bet you know how it
feels.

The calls of the vendors selling coffee or tea–
As the train draws into a station, we peer to see,
Is it a junction or just an interim stop,
We rush to fill our bottles to the last drop.

It's meal time again; the others are now friends–
We offer our idlis and the other aunty too lends.
We chat about life and make small talk,
The best way to win the battle of the clock.

Hopping on to the top berth for a good night's
sleep,
The silent train rocking away is a memory to
keep.
It's morning and our destination is almost near,
We bid our goodbyes and check our seats clear.

A Storm in our Hearts

We are but human–
There are those days,
When dark clouds loom,
A storm batters our hearts.

We feel battered and beaten–
Our souls dragged to the depths.
Our thoughts are on a chase,
Why me, why this fall from grace?

Sometimes we wallow in that phase–
Oft we bail out to newer shores.
New beginnings, renewed dreams,
Steer us out of the murky, dark hole.

Love

I was, as usual, going my way–
None had anything much to say.
Then, from nowhere, wafted a breeze.
Made me hold my breath and just freeze.

A kind word, a look in the eye–
My heart skipped a beat–Oh MY!
Something stirred way down deep,
I could feel the emotion stir and seep.

I lived, I worked, I smiled, I glowed–
Out of nowhere, an aura flowed.
As the world whizzed merrily past,
I prayed this phase could forever last.

Around me, I could whispers hear–
What's with her, she seems afar, yet near.
Folks around could sense my feel,
I drifted around, my world did reel.

It was a new feel, my spirits were high–
I let go, my heart for once could fly.
Is this real? Is this called love?
I sent a grateful prayer to the powers above.

Luck and love together dawned on me–
A world of different hues I could see.
My heart sang and oft missed a beat,
Love has surely swept me off my feet.

The Lunch Box

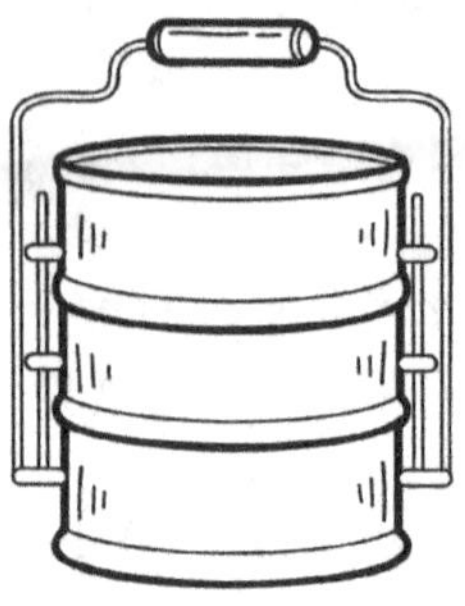

She sends steel boxes filled with love–
My favorite sweets or a simple dish.
I recall my mother's love that I sorely miss,
Ushers in memories of amma's warmth and
love.

The thought that someone truly cares–
To bring me the goodies that I cherish.
Is a gift more precious than the most precious,
My heart wells with gratitude and a silent prayer.

It's not riches that warm the heart–
Kind, thoughtful acts build strong bonds.
We cherish such priceless acts of love,
Wish we could endorse mankind's humane acts.

Word Wounds

The sting of the words,
Sears through our hearts.
Deeper than a spear,
Deadlier than a bullet.

The unhealed scars,
Fester the sinking soul–
Breaks beautiful bonds,
Leaves us bent and broken.

Time heals, they say–
Not the word wounds.
Like the dormant volcanoes,
The pain erupts again and again.

If only we could filter and process–
The might of our words,
We could build everlasting bonds–
Usher in cheer and nurtured love.

A Lazy Day

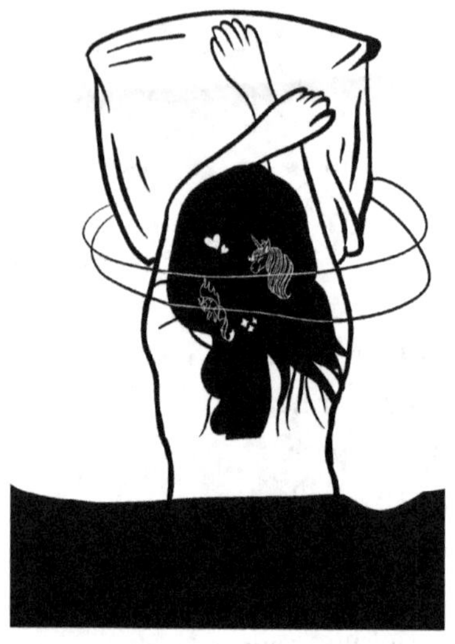

It's another day–
They are all the same.
I cook, I clean, I teach,
Am sapped and drained.

Not today again–
Why be the same?
No chores, no work,
No mails or calls.

No pots nor pans–
No brews, no soups.

I laze, I plod, I dream, I binge,
My favorite pizza delivered.

I read, I nap, I wonder–
Oh! The joy of doing nothing.
Me and myself are great company,
I cherish such lazy days.

Being Human

Not so long ago–
We cared and shared.
What has derailed us–
That we ceased to care?

Everyone seemed in mad haste–
No time to think nor to pause,
Heading to that somewhere,
On a journey to nowhere.

Prisoned within the soulless blocks–
Toiled folks with fluid dreams.
Inside homes were little ones,
Alone with their solo games.

Sincere smiles have sadly waned–
True love has fleetingly flown,
Amidst the madding crowd,
All drifted – all alone.

He

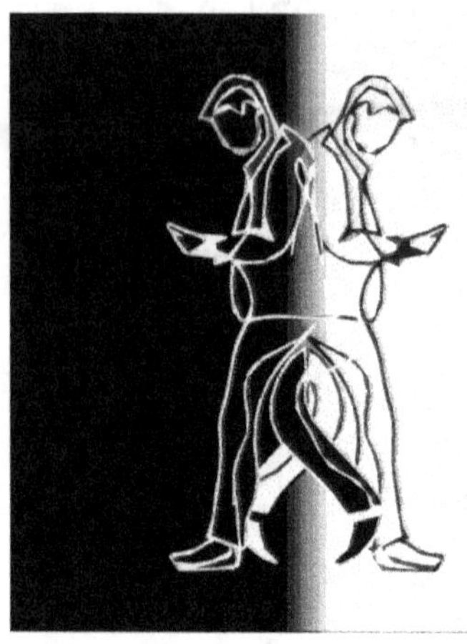

Life was good–
Quite calm and peaceful.
The mornings came,
The evenings and nights too.
Life was the same–
Today and tomorrow.
She sailed along,
With not much sorrow.
Then from nowhere–
He breezed into her life.
At first it was a mere flutter–
Then the wind rose,
And a storm is now raging–
Throwing her across life's shores.

The beatings are painful–
She tries in vain,
To gather herself–
Restore her sanity,
Salvage her soul
And just be herself–
Devoid of emotions,
Numbed by pain,
Marooned in a loveless life.
Again.

In Two Minds

Sometimes I am deft, most times not–
I plod and probe and reach nowhere.
To go or not to go somewhere,
When my heart says nay, my mind says yes!

I consult, I toss, even google–
Nothing helps; I am still in the same spot.
At times, I go halfway and retreat
Then wonder if I should have walked the path.

It's not always this way or that–
More so when I have meals to cook.
I am certain and surprisingly sure,
Of the five-course meal, I love to churn.

In a classroom, I feel like a queen–
No doubts, no qualms – it's my place.

My students and I are on a ride,
Nothing ambiguous at my place of pride.

Learn to Smile

Like the face that launched a thousand ships–
A smile can be your scaffold through hardships.
Wear that smile during good times,
And even more when a failed note chimes.

The power of a smile takes you miles–
Across tough times and grudging guiles.
It's a priceless jewel for the world to see,
Lights up your life with faith and glee.

A smile is so magical it can dissipate–
The biggest hurdles or unbridled hate.
Its power can move mammoth mountains,
Cool a heated moment like dancing fountains.

Learn to smile; it takes you through life–
Has the power to handhold through peril and
strife.
Makes you beautiful and ever so gorgeous,
Spreads power and faith and is so contagious.

A Journey within

There are some days–
We feel out of sorts,
An eerie emptiness shrouds,
Despite a perfect day.

A pull at the heartstrings–
An unexpected stir of emotions,
The sudden whirlpool of loss,
Plunges us into bottomless chaos.

It's time to look within–
Unknot the cluster of thoughts,
Wean the truth from the false,
Declutter our souls, our deeds.

It's always mind over matter–
Clean the cobwebs, arrest the rot,
Make room for happy thoughts.
It's true, peace comes from within.

Childhood

Childhood is a golden phase–
No chores, no goals, no dreams.
We run, we chase, we fall,
We stumble, fail, and rise above all.

School was fun because of friends–
A bit of study and loads of fun.
Not a worry, we just pranced,
Without a pause, we sprinted and danced.

How can we forget the stolen goodies?
The chocolates, the ice cream, and the cakes,

We learned to share with our best friends–
Who are now true friends for life.

Looking back, how badly I wish–
I had stayed longer in those merry times.
How I miss my dear home, my school, my
parents
Who shaped me to stay strong in the race of life.

Let's Appreciate

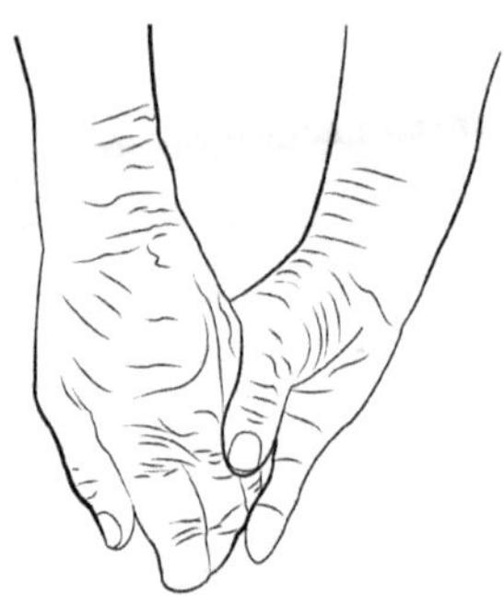

We live in a world–
With opinions aplenty.
Some stay silent,
Some voice out loud.
They all have something to say–
It's oft a critique,
Never a word of praise.

A little accolade–
That bravo pat on the back,
Can be the elixir–
That goads us to go the extra mile.
The world is so mired,
In its own foibles
Has it lost its spirit to appreciate?

Those days

Once in a while, my mind wanders–
To those carefree days of childhood.
The friends, the family, the known, and the
unknown,
Who touched and coloured the canvas of life.

Once in a while, my mind wanders–
To the warmth of my loving home.
The aroma of my mother's cooking,
And the chatter of my sisters.

Once in a while, my mind wanders–
To the childish, simple joys of life.
The echoes of the school bell,
The scurrying boots across my school corridors.

Once in a while, my mind wanders–
To the silly dreams and eager hopes.
The teachings, the discipline in school
The anxious days of exams and results.

Once in a while, my mind wanders–
To the not-so-long-ago times,
When life played different tunes–
I sure learnt from life's past cues.

What's love?

What is love?
Is it a condition–
That prevails,
Or an infection–
That spreads.
Maybe a virus
To watch out.
A distress–
A pipe dream?
An oasis–
That is a mere mirage
A truth–
That's really a lie?
A path–
That leads nowhere
An ache–
That never goes away?

A disease–
Without a cure?
A storm–
That never dies.
An emotion–
That leaves you drained.
A torrential storm–
You wish hadn't come your way.
Yes, the list is long–
And I am still wondering,
Oh dear!
What really is love?

My Parents

The brightest stars in the horizon of my life–
My dear parents were a handsome pair.
The love they had for us and each other,
Made home a haven to nurture.

They sailed through storms and made it–
A model lesson on resilience for us.
Simple lives and supreme values,
The perfect launchpad for us to take off.

The love they shared was epic–
Their gentle ways are still talked about.
My mother's food has left a mark,
So has my father's seamless teaching.

They were the epitome of selfless love–
A model pair is so hard to find.
How I wish they were still around,
To see my journey and read my **'Verses from
Life'.**

Small Joys

In the melee of life–
We forget to look around.
The sunshine fades,
The moon dances in silence.

There is abundant chatter–
All about struggles and battles.
None pause to admire the dew drops,
Dancing on those fragrant petals.

Hold on, pause, look around–
The beauty in nature beckons.

Why miss these blessed moments,
That lend a tinge to the canvas of life.

Shake off that needless dread–
Rejoice amidst the small joys.
Look out for those little moments,
That go unnoticed, unseen.

We don't need to win big battles–
To place our lives on the coveted mantle.
A child's cry, a mother's call, a bird's song,
Are the small joys that goad us on.

The Saga of the Escalator

I saw people glide up–
Saw them glide down as well.
Ah! That's so cool – no stairs to trudge,
Or so I thought at the very first glance.

I got near, was about to step in–
The gnawed metal steps swiftly moved,
In tune with the metallic banister–
There began my escalator Zumba.

A passerby in all goodwill–
Offered to guide and hold,
Until I stepped on and got a hold.
Sadly, he gave up, without my maiden step.

I traveled across seas, the saga followed–
A crowd of willing helpers I surely drew,
Much to the annoyance of those dear,
Escalators are not for me, I vowed.

And then I landed in Dubai, the king of lands,
I gazed in awe at the mammoth towers.
The malls, the sights, the gardens, the food
Took me to a place beyond heaven on earth.

My deadly fear followed me to a majestic mall–
Sheepishly, I confessed to my host and friend.
Without much ado, she grabbed and dragged.
And there was I, on my first ever escalator
Zumba.

Touching Lives

In the magical journey of life–
We mingle with the known, the unknown,
Our paths cross, our lives merge–
Setting the stage for a new bond.

Some are fleeting passersby–
A few shadow us through life.
An unseen hand leads through trials
Together, we wade and win battles.

Out of nowhere, they board our lives' wagon–
On a journey of joy, tears, and love.
We cry and rejoice with and for each other,
Blessed are those who touch our lives.

What do I want?

I look around and wonder–
Should I be here or yonder?
Battles were fought and won,
Yet, there's a void I can't shun.

I peek beyond, at another world–
My old dreams faded and blurred.
Should I choose a newer path–
Filled with love, no war or wrath?

I know not what my heart painfully pines–
How I wish I could read between the lines.
What do I want, what does my heart seek,
I wish I could rewind and look for a new peak.

Maybe it's time to change and shift–
Erase those memories that create a rift.
For sure, I seek the tender rays of love,
I turn with hope to the powers above.

A Rainy Evening

I loved those rainy days–
The claps of thunder deafening,
The lightning lit the swaying garden,
A medley of bird calls and froggy croaks.

The fragrance of the jasmine–
Merged with the dancing lilies.
The earthy smell after the first rains,
Was a treat for my long-parched soul.

My mother's unwaning warmth–
Her rainy day specials brewing,
Merged with the dance of Gods
Filled my rain-soaked drunk soul.

A song in my heart

I sat by the seashore–
And gazed at the blue sky.
The birds flew by,
As the day faded away–
There was a song in my heart.

I saw the children chase–
Run, hide, and seek.
Their screams and laughter
Filled the evening air–
There was a song in my heart.

There sat the old and the young–
Lost in thoughts,
Of the days gone by,
And the coming morrows.
There was a song in my heart

The sun had long set–
The colors of the day faded,
The waves gently lapped the shore–
Only shadows left to see,
There was a song in my heart.

Friends

In the journey of life–
We aren't alone.
Our first friends are at home,
Parents, siblings, and other family.

Then we step out and meet–
Some in the passing,
Some forever to stay,
As an extension of ourselves.

Lucky are those with friends––
To share our woes and extend care.
Halfway along the journey
Some stay, some fade away.

They hold our secrets–
Our lives are an open book,
They are the wall to lean on,
When the world crumbles around.

We cherish them, we look out–
Have each other's back.
We celebrate our wins–
Hold hands when we falter or fall.

Build those beautiful bonds–
They are the rainbows after a storm.
Stay true, be warm,
Friends are the jewels of life.

The Aftermath

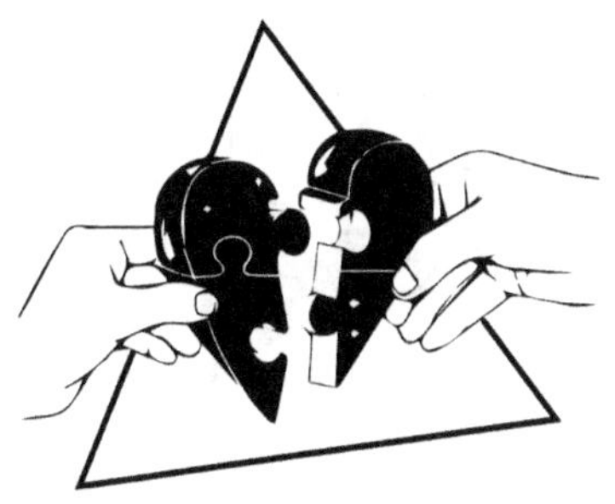

They say love hurts–
I didn't know how,
Until now.
The pain sears–
Through my heart,
Leaves me wounded–
Helpless and worthless.
I drift around now–
Like an anchorless ship
Looking for a mooring
That will ground me–
In a land of peace.
A place where I am numb–
Where there is no hurt.
No tears or emotions,
A place so tranquil–
That I would never
Want to leave,
because there's no love there.

Then and Now

Life raced by, a today and then a tomorrow,
It all felt the same – a little joy and some sorrow.
Life and the living drifted by; as did I
Waiting for that great moment to come by

Oft I looked back at those beautiful days,
My mother's care and father's simple ways.
Those were days filled with laughter
There were no dreams or goals to go after.

Come what may, I have never seized to smile,
A glimmer goads me to that extra mile.
Just when I think, Oh wow! Life is so great
Karma dances in with a twist of fate.

Hang on, I say to my dwindling hope,
An unseen hand leads me as I slip and grope
I see just a faint flicker, a gentle glimmer
I haul myself up, bring it on – I am a winner!

Belief is Power

There are times when we are ready to fly–
No qualms, no fears – we don't even try.
Our spirits soar, there sure is a surge,
With ease, we mingle and deftly merge.

We fly high, way above the clouds–
View the rest beneath the shrouds,
The world we lived, seems far away,
A sudden jolt and there's the dreaded sway.

We come crashing along with our dreams–
Land on a rubble of shattered moonbeams.
We grope, we struggle, look for a hand,
None hear our cries; on our own we stand.

The jolt is harsh, no respite or relief–
Change gears, turn paths – it's our belief.
No time to wallow, moan, and groan.
Rise above the ruins, a new avatar is set to be
shown.

Homeland

There's something in the air–
The wafting aroma from homes.
The waltz of the lush coconut trees,
The rhythm of the dancing ocean.

Even the crows looked grander–
The folks seem filled with pride.
The roads stretched longer
The hues on the horizon are brighter.

And then the familiar haunts–
That morphed my million memories,
My school, that seamlessly shaped,
My friends, my soulmates, still with me.

Oh, and my beautiful home–
Memories of my most loving parents.

The silly squabbles with siblings.
A salute to my heavenly homeland.

How I wish...

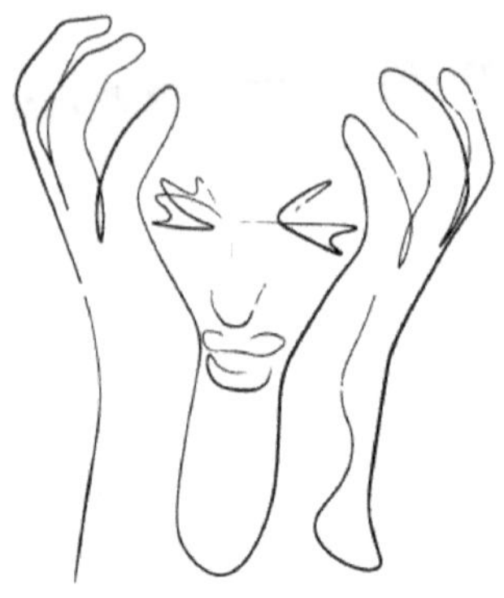

How I wish I could go back in time–
To the warmth of my home,
And relive those pleasant moments,
That we forgot to notice or cherish.

How I wish I had grabbed that moment–
That knocked at my door and was surely mine
I took the wrong road and ended nowhere
A lost chance I regret and moan.

How I wish I had guarded my words–
The fire in them seared my loved ones
Pity I can't retrieve or recall
The hurt is done, and the wounds are raw.

How I wish my dear parents were around–
Pity I couldn't take them around the world,
I wish they could read my Verses from Life,
And I could seek their blessings again and again.

It's a New Dawn

It's a new dawn–
It's the end of days gone,
Perhaps the beginning–
Of a new lease.
A new challenge,
A much-needed change–
Of a new dream,
End of turmoil–
Time to redeem.
Opening new doors
To untrodden paths.
End of a nightmare
A new friendship,
Closure of another.
A peep into the future-
An assessment of self,
A path to penance-
Foray into a new realm,
Forget the past-
Live the day,
It's a new dream-
It's a new dawn.

My Foibles

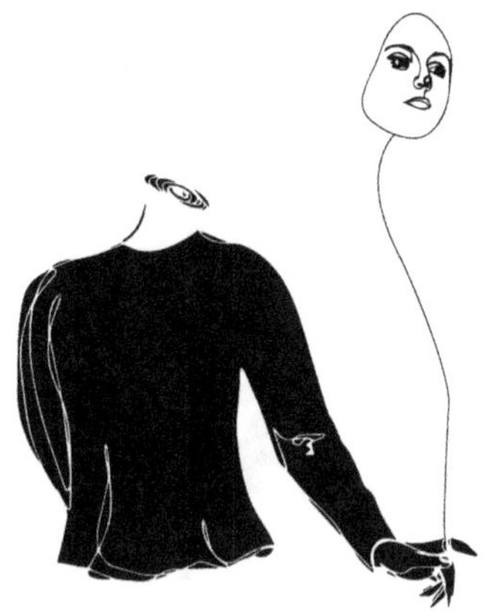

I am perfect amidst the imperfections–
The silly fears, the heightened dreams.
Oft the fears and the dreams cross paths
Then I fall, shaken but not broken.

People call out, isn't she silly?
Even so, I trudge, I hang on.
I reflect on those flaws, learn, and grow,
There's time to mend on my own!

Looking back, I wonder how far I have gone–
I made it thus far despite the foibles.
The road ahead is jagged and pitted–
Life has its flaws too, like I do.

Allow me to fit in, in my own corner–
Let me be the way you outwardly see.
Within me lies my strength, my power,
That can lift me clear of my foibles.

Countryside

The vast expanse of the countryside–
The lakes and the streams gushing by,
The palm and the coconut swaying around,
The squirrels scurrying up and down.

A little beyond was the only school–
Where children played and stayed safe.
Under the banyan sat several folks,
Who cared to share, but listen more.

The neatly lined homes looked alike–
The cobbled roads led you there.
The lovely women laughed and talked,
All seemed happy and at peace.

The vibrant green fields stretched far beyond–
Their vast expanse soothed the hearts.
There was no hurry and nothing to worry,
All seemed to be embraced in eternal love.

Failures

Growing up, we raced for the grades–
The toppers towered above the rest.
The average and the rest lingered and wondered
What's the mantra to scale to the top?

Times have changed, and so have the dynamics–
It's okay to fall, fail, falter, or trail.
The paths to fame are more diverse.
There's a piece of the success pie for you and
me.

History reflects the saga of failures–
From Einstein to Lincoln, we have heard–
The struggle for power or unrequited love,
The race for success or simple inner peace.

For sure, failures are the perfect prelude–
To the train of victories that soon follow.
If not for failure or unreached goals,
Success would lose its sheen and grandeur.

Forgiveness

A war of words, acts of wrath–
Crumble our bonds, haunt our hearts.
A link is severed, a dear one parts,
We are mired in the aftermath.

We sometimes pine, sometimes regret–
Flashes of good times race through our minds.
We reflect, we recall, and go through the grind,
Years of memorable moments, hard to forget.

Let's shed our egos, extend a hand–
Rebuild the bond, try to fix and mend.
A sorry note straight from the heart, let's send,
Without these bonds, where would we stand?

Live in the moment

Live in the moment, they say—
I do, but oft my mind travels,
To those lovely early days—
When I was chirpy and cheerful,
More agile and more alive.

Live in the moment, they say—
I do, but oft my mind travels,
To those warm, carefree days,
With my buddies, my mates
When I was a free spirit.

Live in the moment, they say—
I do, but oft my mind travels,
To those painful heartbreaks,
When I parted with someone special,
My heart aches to this day.

Live in the moment, they say–
I do, but oft my mind travels,
To those lost dream moments
That I failed to make my own,
And freeze those priceless memories.

Pani Puri of Life

Every Indian, across the nation–
Loves his pani puri at all times.
Be it a hot summer day or a stormy one,
A platter of pani puri sets the stage.

The crunch of the plain-looking puri
Sings a duet with the dressed filling within.
Our hearts join the stately chorus,
As the puri slips into our watering mouths.

I have often wondered and pondered–
What's it that makes PP so special?
I bet it's the potpourri of spices
That blend with the chutneys, sweet and sour.

When the potato, chickpeas, and onion team up–
With the mint and coriander, it's no wonder,
This street food in every corner of the nation,
Takes our taste buds on a trip to heaven.

Life for sure is a reflection of our much-loved
pani puri–
It's an amalgam of the sour and the sweet.
Let's embrace every moment with love and zest,
And dance to the rhythm of the flavors of life.

Is it Fate?

When the going is good–
you pat on your back.
The wishes pour in,
Life seems on track.

Then there is a bad day–
Things go swiftly south
And so does your spirit.
There is none to lead the way.

Now begins the blame game,
It's your karma; it's your fate.
You gave it all; you are not to blame,
And now it's far too late.

Why blame fate?
Face life with grace.
Let's begin the chase,
To redeem and swiftly rise again.

Memories

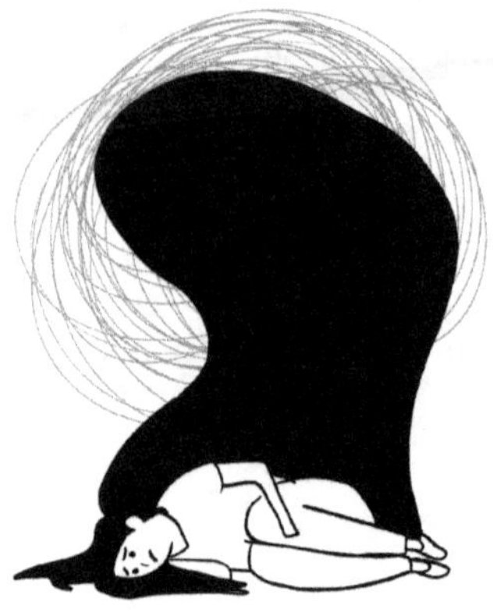

Isn't it strange–
How a fragrance, an aroma
Takes us to the past–
To those fun times
And some that we dread.
To that someone we loved–
And wished was with us
Isn't it strange how
Our memories mend or bend us?

Isn't it strange–
How as the clouds meet
And the rain in vain
Tries to cleanse the pain.
And that rainy day long ago–

Brought cheer to our weary hearts,
Just as life passed by.
Isn't it strange–
How our lives are crafted by our mundane
memories?

Isn't it strange–
How a song from somewhere,
Plays on our heartstrings,
Takes us to those good times,
When there was fun–
With those loved ones–
Now gone forever.
Isn't it strange–
Our memories are the pulse of our lives?

The Canvas of Life

The vast expanse of the world–
The varied tints, the vibrant folks,
Blend seamlessly into the contours,
Of cultures, traditions, and values.

The hearty greetings, the embrace of love–
Binds us despite the conflicts and wars.
Why divide, why differ, we are one,
Reach out –- our dreams are the same.

It's time to reset, time to heal–
Break the barriers and surge ahead
Let the egos fade, usher in the binding bond
Together we heal, a rainbow of hope we see.

The Two of Us

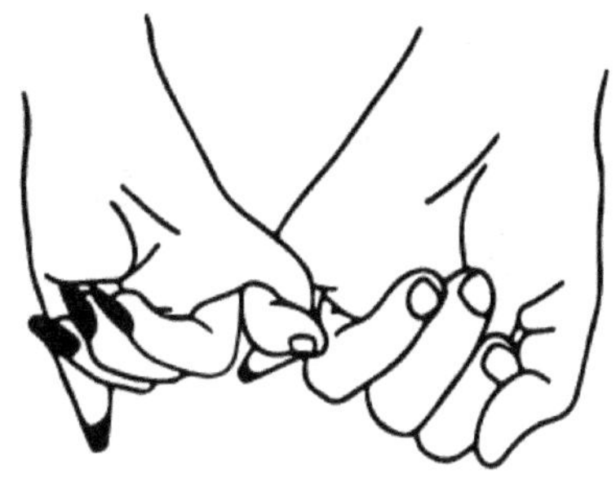

Above all–
We love unconditionally
Give freely
Share happily,
Help wholly,
Laugh heartily,
Feel deeply,
And at times, get–
Confused unnecessarily
Hurt painfully
Misunderstand childishly
Lose miserably
Speak openly
Connect wrongly
Yes, we are the same
Ultimately!

The Unknown

In the journey of life–
Some we meet, some we greet.
Some slip by, unnoticed, unheard,
Some tower above the common herd.

We know not their form–
Nor where they hail from.
Like a shadow, they linger out there,
You know they are somewhere.

By a strange twist of fate
They become your buddy, your mate.
It doesn't need validation, a name,
They are family, you feel the same.

As strange as it may sound–
Such friends are strongly bound.
They look out for each other,
Unlike 'true' friends who are seldom around.

Their hearts send out a prayer,
Wishing health and peace for each other.
They herd together, a friendly fond,
Lucky are those who weave such a bond.

Look out for those special ones,
Who stand out as life swiftly runs–
Ready to extend a helping hand,
That's as magical as an angel's wand!

Feeling Lost

People mill around us–
Yet, invisible they seem,
We are lost in a trance–
Days fleet, months drift.

We linger in our eclipsed life–
There's no jubilance or joy.
Others wander wearily around us,
We sometimes sink, sometimes float.

It's a phase for most of us–
Life's googly oft hits us hard.
We drift around in a deprived daze,
Oft we meet others in the same maze.

Some stay longer in the dark pit–
Some break out and reset.

Life is never easy or smooth sailing,
Let's not be harsh on ourselves for failing.

Path to Nowhere

In the melee of life's streets–
I trudged along solo.
The shrill laughter
And the piercing cries,
Echoed around in my soul.

Some passersby glanced–
Few for a moment paused,
Many just fleeted by–
Dazed and lost in their trance.
No smiles nor hugs, simply pranced

Somewhere, I stopped–
For a breather, some fresh air,
As folks raced on with no care.
Oh no, this is hardly fair
Race to the finish, I dare.

I passed by leafless trees–
And flowerless bushes,

Soulless folks with withered wishes,
To a boundless mirage
In the depths of nowhere.

Solitude

Amidst the noise, betwixt the clutter–
I wish I could be somewhere with none,
To crawl into that heavenly shell of solitude,
To meet my crippled soul – all alone.

Too much laughter and baseless banter–
Crush my wronged and wringed out heart.
I wish I could find a marooned corner,
Away from the dismal days and battered bonds.

I wish to ponder, look back, reflect–
Erase the wrongs, heal the hurtful wounds.
A place to rewind, and meet myself alone,
To pause, ruminate, heal, and reset.

The Pursuit of success

Is it a myth or a fairy tale?
We spend all our life in its quest.
A dream that beckons but eludes,
A lucky few land on the shores of success.

All through life, the search goes on–
We seek, we strive in its search.
Wish there was a mantra for success,
A proven formula or even a masterclass.

Some pundits say it's a mirage–
Why this chase for the elusive?
It's transient and never permanent,
One day it's yours, the other it's gone.

The quest

Every heart yearns–
All souls pine,
For that abstract fulfillment–
Called love.
Some say it is out there,
Some find it nowhere.
Many look for it,
Hither and thither–
And wander around,
Life's alleys seeking–
That faint flicker,
To light up their hearts.

How illusory is love–
That eludes even the Gods.
Peer within and find–

That elusive emotion called love.
And then there are some–
Who swear love is a myth
That doesn't even exist.
Its pursuit is futile–
Love yourself is their call,
You are your master
You are your soulmate.
Why wander in vain?

The deeper you search,
The murkier your journey becomes.
Is love overrated?
Does it even exist?
Lucky are the ones
Who have found it
In the little acts of life
That brings cheer to their heart
And heartens their souls.
Let's not wander and be lost
In the pursuit
of the pipe dream – called love.

Forgotten moments

Out of nowhere, a picture from the past–
Ushers in the priceless moments we wish had
last.
The storm that rainy night, when we huddled,
As lightning lit mother's garden, swaying and
puddled.

A bird song brought to our dreary mind–
The secret love note that we hid and couldn't
find.
A church bell afar ushered in memories of hope,
The answered prayers while on a desperate
slope.

The wafting aroma of coffee brought memories
of mother–
Her priceless love, that we failed to see or
bother.

A Rajesh Khanna song sprang love in our young
hearts,
That we wish had acknowledged and not just
played our parts.

Why do forgotten moments always hurt and
haunt?
We hardly have anything to proudly rave or
flaunt.
Let's paint beautiful pictures with vibrant tinges,
The past memories are where our future hinges.

It's never too Late

The clock ticks, days fleet–
A debris of dreams strewn behind.
We wish, we hope, we pine.
For a new start, a new dawn.

Some say, sadly, it's game over–
Pointless to look back and whine.
New beginnings are not for you,
You are far too gone, don't you pine.

The brave hearts, switch gears–
Choose to walk the path.
The going gets tough, yet they go,
To top up their lives with new dreams.

Then begins a saga so far untold–
Accolades and wins come their way.
New peaks, untold challenges overcome.
Believe me, it's never too late.

The Peak and the Pit

The going is good; there is a spring in our step–
Friends and family greet and meet.
Celebrations and wishes pour,
The cup of joy filled up to the brim.

New horizons emerge, more glory glimmers–
We smile, we cheer; it's all happy banter.
We rise above many, settle right up there,
Time to rejoice, perched on the peak.

We look down at those down there–
Pity they couldn't clamber to the top.
Life down there seemed troubled, but happy,
They had their moments and cheering too.

One wrong move, we are suddenly shaken–
What a blow! Why didn't we see it coming?
The slide begins and things go south
Downhill was for sure, sudden and quick.

We are alone; where are the friends, the family?
The fame, the name are gone with the wind.
We land in the pit, crushed and forlorn,
Somewhere, there's a whisper – it's your karma.

When the World says you can't do this

Be your own coach and cheerleader–
Goad yourself and shape your path.
Plot your dreams and plan your goals,
Even when the world laughs at you.

Strange are the ways of the world–
They make great critiques, not mentors.
Shut the world out, listen to your heart,
Grab your chances, harness your hopes.

The pitfalls and pit stops are painful–
Pause, take a breath and surge ahead.
Recall, the popular, much-heard saying–
When the going gets tough, the tough get going.

Take your time, cross your bridges–
Manifest your dreams, your conquered goals.
Be a torchbearer to the weary world,
And take them along your splendid sojourn.

Dreams do Come True

Growing up, we were often taught and told–
Dare to dream, however hard it may seem.
Chase them, work on them — no matter what,
Rise above the rest, we were constantly taught.

For some, it's a breeze, they make it big–
For most, failures are stepping stones.
It's often step after step, leading nowhere,
Until they give up and crumble somewhere.

Looking back, I guess I am beyond lucky–
My poems were oft an outpouring,
Of the good times and my daring dreams,
I have indeed, come a long way with my **Verses from Life!**